Praise for *Ghosts of the M*

Here in these powerful new poems that make up *Ghosts of the Monadnock Wolves*, Andrew Krivak presents those haunting, scintillant images he gave us earlier in *The Signal Flame* and *The Bear*. A wilderness drumming in the shadows of the Monadnock range, with its unforgiving ice, its Dantesque slopes, and the howl of those ghost wolves and coyotes. In the end, it's a father's hope to somehow protect one's children against those nightmarish forces we know are beyond our control.

Paul Mariani, author of *Crossing Cocytus* and *The Great Wheel*

Andrew Krivak's collection, *Ghosts of the Monadnock Wolves*, celebrates the history of a place in the only way that matters — by giving us the people of the place. In "Lake Ice," there's a passage that suggests his method of poetic exploration: The narrator and his children stand on a frozen lake and watch the "auger as it turns and searches, turns and searches through each frozen layer, until water so green and cold it looks oily gushes up and settles into slush around our boots." Krivak's close eye for the sensory detail grounds all of these poems, and the work reminds me of Harry Humes and the early poems of James Dickey. Reader, get ready to be immersed, get ready to learn what the auger can find.

Charles Rafferty, author of *A Cluster of Noisy Planets*

Ghosts of the Monadnock Wolves

Copyright © 2021 by Andrew Krivak

Cover image by Andrew Krivak
Author's Photo by Sharona Jacobs
Edited by Mark Blackford
Cover design by James Rawlings and Teresa Snow

All rights reserved. No part of this publication may be reproduced, distributed or transmitted in any form or by any means, including photocopying, recording, or other electronic or mechanical methods, without the prior written permission of the publisher, except in the case of brief quotations embodied in critical reviews and certain other noncommercial uses permitted by copyright law. For permission requests, write to the publisher at the email address below.

Chestnut Review
Ithaca, New York
www.chestnutreview.com
ISBN: 9798491311545

Ghosts of the Monadnock Wolves

Andrew Krivak

Chestnut Review Chapbooks

Once more, to Amelia

CONTENTS

Prelude 1

No Great Thing 7

Lake Ice 8

Nocturne, Birchtoft 10

The Way Beavers Swim 11

Road's End Horses 13

Hawk Passing 14

The Ballad of the Coyote Killer 16

Hewers 23

Children Sleeping Out, August 26

January Twelfth 29

The Trail Down 31

Acknowledgments 36

About the Author 37

Prelude

There is a story passed down in the family
Of our grandfather who died in the Lehigh Valley
Breaker, January 1929, robbing the pillars,

A twist of mining in which the last to leave
The emptied seam took with him at the swing
Of a sledge the columns that braced the roof

When he retreated with his butty up the slope.
He never made it out, but they say he tossed
His hammer to a third, and that man used it

To pry up and back the slate and anthracite
That trapped them, found the shaft, and got help.
My father's memory began with that end,

The boy of three growing up in Shenandoah.
There was the rush of cold, the view of the Blue
Mountain from the front window torn out

To get the casket in, and he slipping from
Room to room, listening for the man's voice,
But hearing only his mother's and the Russian

Priest chanting the *Panakhida* for the dead.
That is why my father settled in
The mountains of Pennsylvania after the war

And not the towns that grew along the floodplain
Of the Susquehanna River. He became a hunter,
Kept shotguns and rifles, and I once watched him

Shoot a squirrel through the neck from the bottom
Of a hickory that grew to the height of two homes,
Taking aim only with a bead-and-foresight .22.

To us the city was an unknown world away.
And yet I found it. Drawn to it, even as a boy,
Taking the bus to Wilkes-Barre in the years before

The flood, and moving to New York when
The time came. Once, standing for a long time
Before Hopper's *Pennsylvania Coal Town*

In a museum, I gazed at the painter's vision
Of a place he likely never knew. The benign
Labor of a man painted in a light that means

This cannot be any day other than the Sabbath.
The stark planter out front that wants the light.
And the steps of concrete fashioned and shaped

To show great care. No sign of dirt or disrepair
Anywhere. The man himself seems tasked to
Do no more than draw a rake across the grass.

It was then I noticed an old woman beside me,
Weeping, so, I began to speak to her, not out
Of concern but belief that a story at that moment

Might console her grief. And I told her about
The beginning of the end of mining below
A city and towns built above them on the river.

How in '59, thirty years after my grandfather's death,
Four miners working a vein too far west beneath
The Susquehanna punched a hole into the river's

Floor, and when the flood of water, mud, and boxcars
To clog it ceased, the river left her mines and miners
Buried there, three hundred miles inland, at sea.

That same foreshadowing and loneliness seems
To shroud Hopper's half-lit street, I said.
And in a shift of mood the old woman confessed

(each of us, it's clear now, unburdening)
That she, too, was born in Wilkes-Barre,
And used to walk with her mother across

The bridge on Market Street to eat a bag lunch
On the banks of the river along the dykes,
And stare east through that distance at a finer

Portrait of the town, while the river,
Unnavigable and slow, snaked like an old,
Patient beast. One evening she was surprised

To find a gull perched on rock among bulrush
Near the shore, until she spooked it and the bird
Alighted but remained close by, flying in half-

Circles as though it had been roused with one
Hundred others on a beach. Why did it come
This far, she wondered? Lost. Returning.

I didn't have an answer, and before I could
She said, *It's always both, young man, origin*
and end balanced at their meridian.

We said no more to each other and parted.
And later that night, walking across town
To the Upper West Side, I remembered

That I had asked my father once when I was
Young why there were no boats on the river.
And he said it was too shallow. He said that

If I wanted boats, I had to follow the course
Away from the coal town to where the river
Pours its broadening silt at Havre de Grace,

Then keeps going farther, into the Chesapeake.
Or east, over the Pocono Mountains and lakes
To the Palisades, where the land ceases

On the shores of the Hudson estuary that flows
To the sea, where I'd find everything I dreamed
And loved and recognized as home

Surrounded me no longer, and was held up
In my memory by columns of my leaving,
Which appear benign and resting and shaped

To show great care, until one is taken,
Then another, and another, and the night sky
Above groans starless and threatening, and

There is no time left to find a place of safety
Before the handle of a hammer is all we have
With which to reach and prop up what

And whom we love in that last moment of work.
I think of him here in these mountains, my end
Closer now than my origin, and I walk these trails

Along the spine of a range older than cities,
Painted by those who had come from the city
For rest. Sounds on the air are from redtail hawks

And the mournful call of loons. Scent of pine.
The breeze brings with it mountain weather.
And I am old in an old land I have never known,

Yet have always known since I was a boy
And my father taught me how to live
Off the land, where everything can be found

In the making, in the walking, picking up
And putting down again like feet that scan
These verses. *I swore I would not die from having*

gone down underground, he said to me when he was
The age of the woman I had met in that museum,
Closer to the end than the origin, long past

The meridian. Sunset brings a palette
Of reds and yellows to the clouds in the west,
Deepening from behind the mountain.

Tonight, darkness means there will be a limitless
Canopy of light from the stars. And I will lie
Down and sleep beneath the roof of them.

No Great Thing

Created suddenly. No deep
Benthic zone filled
In the space of a dog's snore.

No white pine covering
The forest's O with cones
Or shade in one season.

No barred owl learns how
To devour the heads of song
Birds on the day it emerges

Blind and down-covered
From its white egg.
That porcupine you said looked

The size of a small bear cub
Needs more than one
Winter gnawing at the supports

Beneath our porch to startle
Even my beliefs. This should
Be clear each night you stare

At the mountain range in silhouette.
Dark against the twilight.
The oldness still somehow becoming.

Lake Ice

1

In those days, we would emerge in morning at the top of the hill, my brother and I, and trek down that eastern-facing slope, the snow deep, the surface crust thick enough to walk on, our skates tied and dangling chest-to-back, until we reached the same water we had to sneak along in summer at first light to catch huge perch and bass. Come winter, old man Kamont, who owned the land, was less stingy and although he didn't exactly invite us, let us skate with him on that millpond, even shoveling a rink-sized patch for us when a snowstorm covered its cracked-glass surface in the night. That was how we knew, when we came through the trees and out into the field and looked down at the pond, the ice was thick enough to skate on. Once I asked the man (who never spoke except to say *Hello!* as we laced up) how he knew the ice was safe. That day he seemed to put aside the work of mourning the son he'd lost on a hill the Marines had given the number thirty-seven and stared off into the woods. Then, sounding like my father, he said that in the balance of temperature and time, when the cold approaches nothing and days of zero stretch farther and farther apart, there is no ice you cannot stand and skate forever on. *So go ahead, son, before the light fails.*

2

That father and his son were reunited long ago in the fields the ancients believed are reserved for us when the time comes. And perhaps because of him I feel drawn to walking down this hill from our house each winter and stepping out with a mix of caution and the thrill of flight onto the ice. Like a last leaf letting go and drifting onto the cold expanse of white. Do you remember when I first laced your skates and took your hand, and you stood and asked with your own thrill and caution if it was safe? I said yes, gave you a tug, and we were off like children in a storybook. I see the same hesitation in our children, too, mornings I am on the ice and they sprint down the hill after me, step, wait, step a little farther, and holler *Is it safe?* I am holding in my hand the auger that I use to judge the depth of ice and holler back for them to come and find out. And there we stand, huddled in the middle of the lake, summer as far away as another solstice, and watch that auger as it turns and searches, turns and searches through each frozen layer, until water so green and cold it looks oily gushes up and settles into slush around our boots. They are set to charge the shore, but there is no cracking, no collapsing, no falling in around the edge at this fulcrum of our belief and trust. And we skate all day, until the light fails.

Nocturne, Birchtoft

Time was, the shepherd could be seen climbing
The hill that led from Gilson Pond and following
The stone wall into a treeless dusk-blue sky,
His flock of merinos clinging to the filthy

Smell of him and the sound of his voice as they
Ambled over stones and grass and gathered
Into a rock pen no higher than the shepherd's
Thigh. And he would sleep there under stars.

Now, those miles of walls are broken through
In places along the trail, great beech and maple
Rising up to block the summit from the ground.

Not hard to believe this was clear-cut and burned.
Harder to believe this was pasture land,
And wolves stalked ewes in shepherds' nightmares.

The Way Beavers Swim

Two lines of Euclid's breadthless length
    Moving on the longest stretch of pond,
        The wake increasing

In a V like geese will trace across the sky.
    Or tracks of turkey scrawled
        In a snowfield.

This is the signature of the pair who
    Brought down the birch I loved for
        The shade it cast

Along the shore, the lazy curve it grew into
    By sapwood wont, like stars low-arced
        On the horizon,

And I whisper from that shore across the pond
    To them, *I hope the trapper finds you,*
        And regret it.

For he will, patient man, and not with the cage
    They've learned just how to trigger
        But with the snare.

And though the culvert flows beneath the road,
    And hills will not be stripped
        By teeth that work

To keep from growing through their heads,
    I will not see the water cleave
        In this same

Morning wake, transient cipher, liquid stride.
    Perfect line in which there seems
        Written proof.

Road's End Horses

(For Louisa)

run in their U-shaped paddock past
the pond and stones and trees along
the forest, and the ribbon-brightened

fence that cautions there's a small stream
of power that courses through, a herd
I have only glimpsed from the distance

of a window in the barn, but now you
touch, feed, groom, and hold a bridle to,
slip over (gently, I'll wager), and ride

out through the paths and trails and roads
they have walked and trotted on for years
before you arrived, before you were born,

horses with names like Dante and Spirit,
horses that move — anyone could see,
even from a distance — like spirits themselves,

horses I hope you will be able to tell me
when I see you again are as real, yes,
as the dirt you swept and the table you set

for the chance to ride them, for the view
from the saddle, for the feel of the reins
and all creation pounding beneath you.

Hawk Passing

(Loosely after TH)

I sit in the leaves of the bottomland, sharp eyes
Scanning the ground. I must not breathe, not move,
Or I will miss the chance to snatch up in my beak
What blind mouse might come through this duff.

No movement from two hundred feet is lost to me,
And I can close that distance in one second to kill,
And still I could not see the thin fence meant
To keep out geese whose goslings I had eaten.

The squirrel gathering acorns for the winter
At the water's edge looked easy, oblivious, and fat.
I dropped like a stone, claws out and readying,
And that claw creation shaped to snap caught not

The rodent's head but the invisible webbing.
Squirrel flinched but felt only the soft-feathered
Underside of me and jumped back into the woods.
I lay upside down in my shit splashed on a rock.

The sun grew hot and beat down on me the first day.
The second day it rained. On the third day the man
And his wife (who know nothing of hunting and fear
Death) arrived to swim and stumbled upon me.

I was delirious with thirst. They covered my head
And cut my foot free. But when I came to and rose
Into the trees, I could not find balance. I was broken
And fluttered precariously on each wing, afraid

I would fall. Lake below. Forest within reach. I dropped
And angled for the floor I had once scorned. No more.
No more surveying from my perch. No more twist and
Dive and lift out again to live. I rot here like the rest.

The Ballad of the Coyote Killer

1

A boy and his dogs, raised by a father
    To hunt, track fox and
        Bobcat, spring, autumn, winter, raised
            To let them hunt their own

Game of hare, and geese, and beaver among
    The rushes where the springs
        Flow down and empty into the pond all
            Summer and winter.

The deer and bear he killed each year fed him
    And his wife and child
        In the woods he cleared, the cabin he built,
            And the kennel he set apart.

He and those hounds ran with no self-doubt
    Along the mountainside.
        He could touch what he knew, believed
            What he touched, and read

What was written in the record on the ground.
    Read over his barrel scope.
        Populations of the white-tail falling and rising
            On the acorn mast years.

Bobcats selective in the harvesting of rabbits
    From warren to warren.
        The hawk too with its raptor's view appetite
            Finding the movement of mice

And unchanged varying hare in early snow.
    Hunger inescapable in winter,
        The tracks and blood and signs of struggle
            Like the quiet rhythm of

Deciduous trees from season to season.
    So the harsh kills he found
        In the groves and meadows along the path
            Up the mountain lay

Like the disrupted ending of a story once
    Told well, until another
        Teller came onstage and began to play an old
            Part in an Eastern tale.

From those hills one night in spring, months
    Before he saw them, he heard
        The howl and yapping, packs of *canis latrans*.
            Coyote, his father called them,

The name rhyming with *high note*, and told
    Stories of dogs they'd lured
        And killed. All along the mountain, warrens
            Of hares wiped clean.

Sightings and the tracks in snow of deer and bobcat dwindled.
    Still, he knew this was their way.
        So he let them. That was his way. Let them
            Hunt their way.

2

Until the night they loped down the mountain
    And into woods that bordered
        The land on which he had built his cabin,
            And a bitch in heat played

Weak and slinked toward the scent hounds,
    Slid into the pound,
        And lured his lead dog out with her breathing.
            The pack waited

As she pulled the alpha wild with desire
    Toward the woods
        And let it mount her so that it could not
            See the others approaching.

He found his kennel soundless and cowering
    In the morning, and walked
        Behind the smoke house where his lead lay
            Bloodied, disemboweled

And distant-eyed, as though waiting for the man
    Before breathing its last,
        Paw prints and hair tufts telling him what
            The dead dog could not now.

In the house he filled a rucksack, fetched
    His Marble knife,
        And took his rifle from the wall with shells
            And put these in his coat.

He kissed his wife and sleeping child, slipped
    Back outside and said goodbye
        To the pack as they began to moan for the man,
            Their leader lost to them.

He turned his back. Forest paths he knew still
    Led him to the slopes
        That approached the mountain and these
            He climbed until they rose

To cliffs and these too he climbed, hand over
    Hand, the rifle slung around
        His back, his boot-soles all that clung
            To lichen and the granite.

And when he reached the top of the old heights,
    He looked out over all
        The earth that he had known and walked along,
            And listened.

3

Evening was coming on and that was what
    He wanted, to hunt
        At night among those nocturnal hunters.
            Track them, kill them,

Restore the balance within which he lived
    His life. He would not give up
        The high ground he had claimed. He sat among
            Stone in that terrain,

Treeless and amplifying the wind, until
    He heard the notes
        Rising from a cliff he had not known, a cliff
            He had left alone

For its steepness. For its caves. For its drops.
    He heard the same notes
        His dogs far off heard and rose to, wanting.
            He understood the wanting.

It gave up their position, their own need to cry
    Among those stones. And he
        Would not rest, he whispered to himself,
            Until their crying ceased.

Relentless, he drove them from behind the pack,
    Picking off the slow ones as he
        Tracked them up the mountain's saddleback
            And left them on the path.

There were no longer even scavengers that
    Would take their bodies. No,
        They would bloat among the stones now,
            Only rain washing them.

On the third day he saw the last two
        Standing on the ridge
                Waiting for him, he knew, and he levered
                        A cartridge into his rifle,

Shot the bitch to the lead dog's left and watched
        Her tumble over the cliff.
                He put the rifle down, took off his pack,
                      And pulled the knife

From its sheath, without dropping his eyes once.
        They stood at fifty yards,
                Man and dog, and began to approach
                      Each other, slow at first,

Then at a run until they lunged and embraced,
        The man leaning back his head
                To avoid the teeth and plunging his knife
                      Into the coyote's chest.

4

Summer, and I lie out in the meadow
        Among the scent of rose
                Hips and huckleberries, listening to
                      The sound of loons

Ululating on the lake for their own.
        The stars are a crush
                Of light in a lightless sky and only
                      The silhouette of mountain

Draws a curtain on that play of light.
    Insects and fossorial
        The only constant sounds I hear until
            I swear I can make

Out the yap of a coyote in the distant hills.
    Echo or cry,
        I cannot tell. It has been years, and there
            Are no hunters here

To read those same stories along the ground.
    They're ghosts, I tell myself.
        But I know too that revenant means return.
            Others like him do.

I rise to face the curtain facing me and wait
    Like some composer waiting
        For the strains of that polyphony rising.
            Notes, crescendo, dread.

But it is wind over water and in the leaves of trees.
    Acorn hunters rustling.
        These and only these. Nothing else disturbs
            My climb tonight.

Hewers

The trees topped and stripped of their reach
lie like heroic dead. He sights
their length and with the bawling chainsaw bucks

them into stove-length. When he's finished, he finds
a stump, sits down, fills his pipe and holds it
until his hands stop shaking. Then he smokes

and asks how much I think we've got on the ground.
Half a cord? He nods, knocks the pipe
into wet leaves, stands, places a log on

the chopping block and takes up the maul.
The helve brings the head around and the wood
cleaves from some explosion set within.

*

As boys, my brother, a friend long gone, and I
pushed over the beech and pine that died in each
seasonal attack of caterpillars.

We notched the edges deep with hatchets and stacked
them to build a hidden cabin in our woods.
Scornful in the fall that we remained

scavengers of the dead, we took a bow saw
to a tall green hickory and, once the yellow
jackets attracted to the smell of fresh dust

and shavings disappeared, found our hatchets
bounced off the hardwood grain like rubber
balls bounce off blacktop. We left that tree

to season and dry, and in the spring finished
the walls, but never could lift the logs we timbered
high enough over our heads to roof the cabin.

He found it, the hewer, on a walk one morning,
and came back home to get the axe and saw
and set to work reducing in an afternoon

what had taken us three seasons to leave
unmade. *Don't you ever put a blade to good
wood again,* he told us before sleep that night.

*

I was reduced to the clearing and the piling then,
apprentice to the labor, not the axe,
a boy unseasoned watching a seasoned man's

refusal to weaken. A man who one day did.
The explosive *TOK   TOK   TOK* of each
blow when I swing now is like an echo

sent out from the tops of these hills
and does not return, no matter how many years
I swing and wait, swing and wait. The hewer

is gone. My brother too. The way of our friend.
Around me lay a cord of quarter-split oak
and ash that I have worked on since the morning.

Cut your own wood, my father said. *It'll heat
you twice.* He spoke like that. Lived like that.
Protector of all but what he could not.

Children Sleeping Out, August

Afternoon. The beech leaves motionless.
The morning breeze has abandoned us,
gone somewhere to wait out this play
of heat and hush.

Skies threatened an hour ago, and thunder
thumped over the mountain like a drumbeat.
Now there's only that whir in the air cicadas
and mosquitoes make.

The children too are laid low. Drained
of their desire for bicycles, banter, water.
Waiting for the first move of whatever will
in a month like this.

There are times when the counting down
of the hours and minutes in a day comes
as a relief. The longing to let go as strong
as to keep.

So, we rise, walk to the meadow. Against our
shins the touch of grasshoppers and grass stems.
And come to the place. Level and without stones.
Out in the open.

The house looks less like a refuge from the hill.
We each take a corner of the tent and raise
the poles, shake the sides, and stake it down.
It is still too hot,

and we are slow and sweating, but there is talk.
The pecking order that never seems to end.
The tarp floor smells of New Hampshire.
As old as the hills.

The son I told to bring the broom sweeps
the dried grass and insects out the front flap,
and it's as if that very act makes the air itself
move from somewhere to here.

A squirrel scampers across a branch in the woods.
A chipmunk squeaks on a stone, and birds
overhead wing flocked and fast. Evening breeze,
the day changing with us.

In time the sun goes down and stars come out.
Food comes up from the house. Sleeping bags
and blankets lay on the tent floor like overlapping
borders of nations.

There is no light to read by, so I tell them a story
about the dog I had when I was a boy.
And when I'm finished coyotes yip and howl
from the summit.

The youngest is afraid. The oldest tells her they're far
away and won't come into the meadow. I wonder
out loud if it's coyotes, and begin the story
of the Monadnock wolves.

The shepherds who herded sheep on the slopes.
Farmers who built the walls we pass in the woods.
And the wolves who lived on the mountain
a long time ago.

Shepherds and farmers both set fire to the hills
To kill off the wolves. These children have seen
The bald eroded summit. The caves we pass.
Never a wolf though.

And I ask them. Coyotes tonight? Or the ghosts
of the Monadnock wolves, crying still, voices
moving through the night like stars,
and the way that wind will.

January Twelfth

Days of cold
wind, ice, and snow
on the pond so
thick it has become
a road for fox, fisher,

and some rogue night-
hunter whose shoreline
scat I cannot identify.
Day of your birth,
a day I hold still

in my gloved hand
like quiet. Hold as I
would a caught-off-guard
rabbit, slow vole,
or smoky shrew, alive

among the frozen leaf
pack where it will not
become that hunter's
catch. This is the month
in which the kind

find out if they have it
in them to act.
To reach down and
protect the smallest
heart in winter when

lengthening days are no
comfort to the need
to find comfort
from the ice and wind,
months away from thaw.

The Trail Down

...fires ran through it and killed the turf; then the trees were blown down, and their roots turned up and formed a dense and impenetrable thicket in which the wolves abounded.

—Henry David Thoreau, Journal 4:345

1

This granite crest, smooth and tree-bereft.
Chert seams straight as pearlgray streams.
No place to hunker down from the wind and rest.
Not even the ground retreats from it.

You cursed the steep climb all the way up.
I'd forgotten how difficult it is for first timers.
But this mountain is an old fucker
       indifferent to what ails us.

2

Summit pools are cold and clear in autumn.
Algae from the warmer months sinks back into the mud
       that has outlasted fires and rains and day hikers.

Thoreau splashed his face and beard with this water,
       then sat back and looked out over Massachusetts.

3

When the children climbed, all they wanted to do
        at the top was let their jackets billow like sails.
I thought they'd be afraid of being blown off a rock.

Kerouac gives this koan in *The Dharma Bums* —
When you get to the top of the mountain, keep climbing.

Steep and sheer will not describe Monadnock.
Only the word *alone*.
Days shrouded in cloud.

4

When our boys were young, they stared into the rock pools
        and asked where the water goes.
Through dirt and fissures in the stone, then comes up in springs
        on the bottom of Thorndike Pond, I told them.

Look at what water rises from the surface of the earth below.
Trails it takes down the mountain. Trails we will never know.

And Thoreau? one asked.

Imagine a young man on that ledge relieving himself happily,
his own water no different in time from rain and melting snow.

And they vow that day (as children will) not to swim in the pond
        ever again.

5

When I was young, and my father took me to see
Pennsylvania's Grand Canyon, we hiked the trail

down to Pine Creek. In those days you could.
The year was hot and drought-stricken and rattlesnakes

crawled from the forest to the waterside. We ran into some.
Timber rattlers, long and mean and coiled up in their anger

at our trespass. I feared the thought of them.
Feared the sight of them. Feared their sound.

One night, in my dreams, I was bit as I hovered
at the edge of a ravine and wondered what falling

into a grand canyon would feel like?
These moments happen in old lands too.

6

And so, we rose into the wind and set off down the mountain,
    your face still flushed, sweat at your brow.
As much as we tried to descend together, your hand reaching
    for my shoulder, the rocks would not allow it.

I don't know that anyone but I call it the saddleback trail.
But that's what it is, and you found it easier going than the climb.

Thoreau built a cabin with a hatchet somewhere near here
    and slept in it for days while it rained.

We moved to good cover in the trees. Moss on the ground.
You wondered out loud what children have been conceived
   here on the mountain that stands alone?
What names did their parents give them?

A couple came up and over the crest of a boulder, two who looked
   as though they were as familiar with the mountain
   as they were with the years they have climbed together.

Their son is named Henry Birchtoft, they told us, and hiked on.

7

That cool familiar feel of descent.
The touch of breeze. The pines susurrant.

We have dropped into the shade of hemlock groves
that grow taller out of the wind.
A skittish doe crosses our path and we slow
   to let it make its way back into the forest.

One day we will strike the trail and find the caves
   where they say the wolves died.

One day the stone walls we follow now will be hidden
   beneath the falling leaves.

One day we will swim in the last century's rain and snow
   as it too takes the trail down beneath the humus
   and detritus we tread upon without a sound.

One day, beneath the rocks and conifers and deadfall we walk around.

One day, drawing closer, closer, closer to the ground.

Acknowledgments

The author would like to thank the following: Joan Hanley and Thomas Moore for their inspiration and friendship as artists and neighbors, and for telling me the story about the ghosts. Mark Blackford for having shepherded these poems so gracefully onto the page. And finally, Amelia, Cole, Blaise, and Louisa. They are the reason why there is any poetry at all.

About the Author

Andrew Krivak is the author of three novels, a previous chapbook of poems, and two works of nonfiction. His debut novel, *The Sojourn*, was a 2011 National Book Award finalist and winner of both the Dayton Literary Peace Prize for fiction and the Chautauqua Prize. His second novel, *The Signal Flame*, was a finalist for the Chautauqua Prize. His most recent novel, *The Bear*, received the Banff Mountain Book prize for fiction and was also a finalist for the Chautauqua Prize. His chapbook *Islands: Poems* was published by The Slapering Hol press in 1999. As a scholar and a writer of nonfiction, Krivak is the editor of *The Letters of William Carlos Williams to Edgar Irving Williams, 1902-1912,* which won the Louis Martz prize for scholarly research on William Carlos Williams, and the author of the memoir *A Long Retreat: In Search of a Religious Life*. His new novel *Like the Appearance of Horses* is forthcoming in 2023. Krivak lives with his wife and three children in Somerville, Massachusetts, and Jaffrey, New Hampshire. Please visit his website at: www.AndrewKrivak.com.

Made in the USA
Monee, IL
21 March 2025